THE TRUE ACCOUNT OF

Adam & Eve

WRITTEN BY

Ken Ham

ILLUSTRATED BY

Bill Looney

Master Books®

First printing 2012

Copyright © 2012 by Ken Ham and Bill Looney. All rights reserved. No part of this book may be used or reproduced in any manner whatsoever without written permission of the publisher, except in the case of brief quotations in articles and reviews. For information write: Master Books®, P.O. Box 726, Green Forest, AR 72638

Master Books® is a division of the New Leaf Publishing Group, Inc.

ISBN: 978-0-89051-670-6
Library of Congress Number: 2012943105

Unless otherwise noted, all Scripture quoted is taken from the NKJV (New King James Version, copyright © 1982 by Thomas Nelson, Inc. Used by permission. All rights reserved).

Please consider requesting that a copy of this volume be purchased by your local library system.

Printed in China

Please visit our website for other great titles:
www.masterbooks.net

For information regarding author interviews, please contact the publicity department at (870) 438-5288

Master Books®
A Division of New Leaf Publishing Group

DEDICATION

This book is dedicated to the precious children of the world, who all need to hear the wonderful truths from God's Holy Word.

Always Start with the Bible

Before we get started on the true account of human history, look up the following verses in the Bible. This will help you understand that the Bible really is very special. It *is* the Word of God, who *always* tells the truth, and who has always existed. Studying God's Word is the only way we will know the truth about the history of the universe and mankind.

Bible verses: 1 Thessalonians 2:13; 2 Peter 1:19–21; 2 Timothy 3:14–16; Psalm 119:160; Proverbs 30:5–6; Hebrews 4:12; 2 Timothy 2:15.

Here is a verse from the Bible it is good for everyone to learn:

"All Scripture is given by inspiration of God, and is profitable for doctrine, for reproof, for correction, for instruction in righteousness" (2 Timothy 3:16).

Purpose of this Book

This book has been written to instruct readers about the historical account of the first two people, Adam and Eve, and to teach them to think with a Christian worldview that is rooted in the Bible. Adam shows up numerous times in both in the Old and New Testaments. Yet some today try to tell us that Adam was not a real person and despite even Jesus and Paul referring to him, that Adam could not have been real, created by God, and lived in the Garden of Eden as the Bible tells us he did.

Some people also say that the six days of Creation were not ordinary days as we know them, but were long periods of time. When you read Genesis chapter 1, you will see that the word "day" is used with "evening," "morning," and a number for each of the six days. This means they must have been *ordinary* days as we know them. They were not long periods or millions of years. The seven-day week that people accept is based upon the days of God's creation!

You will learn that Christianity is based in real history, and that the Bible is not only a book about salvation, but is *the history book of the universe*. It is the *only* 100 percent accurate history book in the world! Using the Bible, we can learn about the past and also the future. The more you understand about the Bible, the more you will be able to understand and defend the God's truth.

*H*ave you ever imagined what it would be like if you could see the world after God first created it about 6,000 years ago? What would we see? We can't go back to that time—but the Creator of the universe made sure that all the most important events of history were recorded in a special series of books that together make up one book, called the Holy Bible.

One question people often ask is, "Where did humans come from?" Well—let's start at the beginning to find the answer! The Bible starts with a book called Genesis, which means "beginning." That's why God put that book first. When you read a book, you start at the beginning so you understand the rest of the book.

The first verse in Genesis states that God created the heaven and the earth. God has always existed (no one made God, for He made *everything*). God tells us in this first verse that He made time (beginning), space (heaven), and matter (earth). This was the beginning of our universe, all part of the first day in time.

As you read the first chapter of Genesis, you discover that God gives us a summary of what happened on each of the six days of Creation:

> Day 1: time, space, earth, water, light;
> Day 2: preparing the expanse around the earth;
> Day 3: the dry land appeared and God made the plants;
> Day 4: God created the sun, moon, and stars;
> Day 5: God created the sea creatures and the flying creatures;
> Day 6: God created the land animals and the first two people.

The Creation account is also part of Genesis chapter 2 and is a detailed account of what happened on the sixth day—particularly related to the creation of Adam and Eve.

Now, let's take a closer look at what God did on the sixth day. First, God spoke and all the land animals came into being, each according to its kind, which would have included dinosaurs. Pleased with everything that was made, God stated twice that it was "good." He blessed the animals and told them to be fruitful and multiply, giving them wondrous plants and trees with fruit to eat.

God also planted a garden called Eden. Within the garden, God planted two special trees — the Tree of Life and the Tree of the Knowledge of Good and Evil.

Then He made the first man from the dust of the earth, breathing life into him so he became a living being. This man, Adam, was placed in the Garden of Eden to care for it and to keep it. As a test of obedience the Lord gave Adam every tree to eat fruit from, except for one: the Tree of the Knowledge of Good and Evil. Adam was warned that he would die if he ate of that one tree.

Why the rule about this particular tree? God didn't make Adam to be like a puppet—He wanted Adam to love His Creator because he wanted to, not because he was forced to. That's why Adam was given this test. Adam had a choice to obey God or to disobey and create sin in our lives. His choice would affect all of us, as you will learn later in the Bible.

In addition to the beautiful garden that God made, He also brought animals He had created to Adam for him to name. Many scholars feel that God did this so that Adam could see that he was unique, not one of the animals, and during this he realized he was alone—there was no one else like him in all Creation.

This is much different than the evolutionary story that is presented about people. Instead of being special creations made by God, man supposedly evolved from ape—like creatures. But once again, the Bible is very clear. Adam, a real person, was created; a home was prepared for him, and God gave Adam the opportunity to see he was not an animal. God showed Adam he was unique—he was different from the animals, and he didn't have a mate as the animals did.

Some people say that Adam couldn't have possibly named all the living creatures in just one day, so they think the creation of Eve, which occurred after this event, had to take place much later. However, Genesis 2:20 says, "Adam gave names to all cattle, to the birds of the air, and to every beast of the field." It doesn't say anything about his naming sea creatures or creeping things.

Also, "all cattle," and "every beast of the field" (Genesis 2:20) does not mean the same thing as every "beast of the earth" (Genesis 1:24); it was probably a smaller set that represented some of beasts of the earth. Adam only named the animals God brought to him, and besides, he had much of the day to do it.

Before sin, Adam's brain was perfect, so he shouldn't have had problems coming up with names. He could have named all those listed in a few hours. We're not told though how long it was before Adam understood he really was alone!

God said it was not good that Adam was alone and would make a helper for him. He put Adam to sleep to make the first woman from his side, his own flesh:

And the LORD God caused a deep sleep to fall on Adam, and he slept; and He took one of his ribs, and closed up the flesh in its place. Then the rib which the LORD God had taken from man He made into a woman, and He brought her to the man. And Adam said: "This is now bone of my bones and flesh of my flesh; she shall be called Woman, because she was taken out of Man." Therefore a man shall leave his father and mother and be joined to his wife, and they shall become one flesh (Genesis 2:21–24).

Notice the Bible tells us Adam spoke, and revealed his understanding of the importance in how Eve was created from part of him, and how this connection related to marriage — a man and a woman becoming one person.

When teaching that marriage was to be between one man and one woman, Jesus quoted from Genesis 2:24 and also Genesis 1:27:

> And He answered and said to them, "Have you not read that He who made them at the beginning 'made them male and female and said, "For this reason a man shall leave his father and mother and be joined to his wife, and the two shall become one flesh'?" (Matthew 19:4–5).

God gave this first man a specific name — Adam — and Adam named Eve (Genesis 3:20). They were male and female. God did not make two males or two females at the beginning or one man and several females. He made a male and female, representing the first marriage. This is why marriage is only to be one man for one woman.

People were also to have dominion, or basically be in charge; a role given to them by God to look after the creation. Now originally, before sin, this did not mean they could kill or eat animals. No, originally it was a perfect world, and the first two humans and the animals lived in perfect harmony, with man overseeing the creation God made and responsible for its care.

$\mathcal{N}$otice these first two people were made in ways that were unlike all the other created things. What can we learn about the first two humans from how they were created?

1. We were made in God's image. This means humans were different from the animals. Even though we breathe air, live on land, and do many other things like mammals, we are not animals. We can think about our own existence.

2. We were made uniquely to have a relationship with our Creator. God stated that He made them in His likeness, giving them authority over the fish, and the birds, and all things that creep on the earth. Humans were given a role as stewards by God to look after this beautiful world.

As He has for each of us, God had a special purpose for Adam and Eve. They were not an accident, random creation from evolutionary processes, or metaphor for something else. They were people specially created by God to fulfill His plan.

*A*dam and Eve were to have children (only a male and female can naturally reproduce and have children). They would then tell their children about their Creator. These children would one day marry and have children, telling these children about the Creator, and so on.

God wanted people to live long and happy lives. People were to fill the earth and be stewards of it. In a perfect world, they would also be able to interact with their Creator in harmony.

God also made man very smart so he could explore and learn all about the wonders of God's creation. Man could discover more about how great God is, and also understand the natural laws God made so the universe can function. With this understanding, inventions could be developed and reflect our creativity for being made in the image of God. Inventions can make things better in a sin-cursed world.

What was it like to live in this perfect world before sin? People did not kill or eat animals. Animals did not eat other animals or people. Humans were not afraid of animals, and animals were not afraid of humans. Adam and Eve as well as the animals ate only plants and fruit (Genesis 1:29–30). There was no death of animals or people in the world. Try to imagine the most beautiful place you have ever seen, but even that cannot compare to the beauty of the world when God first created it.

Remember when God described everything He made as "very good." This means there was no cancer, no suffering, and no violence. This was the beautiful, perfect world God made for people before sin messed it all up.

NON-STATE B...
COUNTER-TERRORIS...
TERM
CYBER

The Daily Telegraph
Britain's biggest-selling quality daily

War on America

60,000 jobs lost in a single day

THE SUNDAY T...
...ed: the sec...
...uclear...

deep into e...

Abundant pink slips

	Jobs cut in January	Portion of jobs at company
	100.0%	
	9.0	

...sands of workers lose their jobs at mai...
...manufacturing, retail, in...

Have you ever really thought about sin and why things are so messed up in our world? Have you struggled to understand why people get sick or die? People are killed in wars, accidents, and bombings, horrible tragedies like tsunamis and hurricanes occur, and there are diseases, starving people, and many other sad and bad things.

It's a world full of suffering, sickness, sadness, and death. We dig up the bones (fossils) of enormous numbers of animals, including dinosaurs. In many ways it's not a nice world at all. And yet, at the same time, it's a world where there is happiness, beauty, health, and life!

So, what happened? How did the world go from being "very good" to how it is today? Only the Bible has the answer; an all-beautiful, perfect world was messed up by sin! Now there is beauty and ugliness; death and life; love and hate.

Genesis chapter 3 records the saddest event that has ever occurred in the whole of history since the beginning 6,000 years ago. This event changed everything in the entire universe. In fact, this event caused changes for eternity. This is when sin entered the world and with it came death.

Adam and Eve were living in what we would call paradise. God had provided everything they would need. They had no worries, no fears, no challenges; life was perfect. Yet, they still chose to disobey.

There in the garden, the devil or Satan who was a rebellious angel that wanted to be god came in the form of a serpent that spoke to Eve to trick her. He asked her if God had really said that they should not eat of every tree God had made. She remembered the Tree of the Knowledge of Good and Evil, and stated that God had told them not to eat of it.

Here the serpent then twisted God's words and told her that she could become like a god if she would take it and eat it. With this, she took it to eat and offered some to Adam as well. Adam made the choice to eat (I Timothy 2:14), and with that decision, the future of all of Creation would change. Adam had been given the instruction by God not to take the fruit of that tree (Genesis 2:16 and 17) — and Adam was the head of his marriage as determined by God. This is why Adam is blamed for sin, not Eve.

There are people today who try and trick you with questions like the serpent tricked Eve: "Is the Bible really God's Word or merely words written by men?" If you're aware of this trick, you'll be able to stand strong when you hear the question and give the right biblical answer.

Another confusing issue concerns questions about fossils. Don't be fooled when you hear secular (non-Christian or even professing Christian) scientists talking about the fossil record and it is saying millions or billions of years old. Their explanation would have things living and dying, being buried millions of years before man ever "evolved" from apes. This would mean death existed before Adam's sin.

But the Bible is clear about the creation of the world and that death (of animals and humans) came into the world only after sin! So how did all those fossils form? Most of the fossil record is actually the graveyard of Noah's Flood that occurred about 1,700 years after God created the universe.

Are you wondering why sin is such a big deal? How it could cause death and all of these other bad things? Again, the Bible gives us the answer and lets us know God would not let the effects of sin keep us from a relationship with Him, and He had a plan to help us conquer death and have eternal life with Him.

Why would God tell Adam they would die from eating the fruit, yet the Bible tells us they lived? In the original Hebrew language of Genesis, "surely die" means that Adam would start to die, and eventually die.

Actually, Adam died spiritually immediately! The perfect relationship Adam and Eve had with their Creator was broken. And Adam started to die physically the very moment he sinned. We read in Genesis 5:5 that he died 930 years later. In the New Testament, God's Word in Romans refers back to this event when we read:

Therefore, just as through one man sin entered the world, and death through sin, and thus death spread to all men, because all sinned (Romans 5:12).

The Bible also reveals in Romans 8:20–22 that sin affected *everything* God had made. It affected plants, the dirt, the stars, and each human being. *Everything* in the universe. You see, it is important to understand that the bad things that happen in the world are not God's fault! They occur because we rebelled against our Creator! And we now have a taste of what life is like without God.

After eating the fruit, Adam and Eve felt shame and they hid. They also fashioned clothes for themselves out of leaves — hiding from God in guilt. God, who knows everything, asked where they were. Why would He ask when He knew? It was a chance for them to tell God what they had done; it was a chance to repent. Notice how Adam blamed Eve and God, while Eve blamed the serpent. Have you ever done something wrong and lied about it? Or blamed someone else when you got caught doing something wrong? We really do have the same human nature as Adam!

Adam and Eve would not only face the consequences of their actions, but so would the serpent, who was cursed to crawl upon its belly in the dust. Yes, they would continue to live, but their lives would be much harder because they could no longer live in Eden, and they would eventually die.

But the story doesn't end here, because God is about to give Adam and Eve the first clue of how man can once again be in fellowship with God.

We need to understand that God is holy, pure, and without sin. Therefore, God couldn't have the same once-perfect relationship with Adam now that he was a sinner. Adam, who once walked with God, could no longer be close to God in that way. Because we are descendants of Adam, then we have his nature. This means we are like him. He sinned, and so we are sinners.

When Adam and Eve disobeyed God, they sinned. And their sin changed things for all of God's creation, even us!

1. **Sin**: We all sin now and make mistakes!

2. **Pain**: God permits things to hurt now, including child-bearing pain.

3. **Diseases**: from fevers to cancer.

4. **Thorns and thistles**: many plants now have these was a reminder for sin each time we get stuck!

5. **Conflicts**: You don't always get along with people and things don't always work like you planned.

6. **Death**: We will all die because of sin.

7. **Animal death**: our pets and other animals die due to sin as well.

8. **Disasters**: like hurricanes and tornadoes.

9. **Shame**: We are embarrassed of things, especially of being naked in public!

10. **Illogical**: we don't always think the right way about things.

11. **Need**: for a Savior, Jesus Christ to save us from sin and death!

12. **New creation**: We have a need for a new heavens and new earth because this one is cursed and broken.

God killed animals, and took their skins to make clothes for them. Because of their decisions, the first death occurred in God's once-perfect world. Something had to be sacrificed in their place. Why did God do this? He was showing Adam and Eve what death was and that now it would be in the world. Not only would people die, but animals would also die. Remember, sin affected *everything*.

God was also showing Adam and Eve that the animal symbolized a very special person who one day would come and pay the penalty for sin. The final and worst effect of sin would be eternal separation from God (Hell) and God wanted us to live with Him forever!

Surely we would want to live with God in a place without sin for eternity. So what was God's plan to save man from these horrible effects of sin? How could sinful people ultimately be able to live with God — when a perfectly holy God must judge sin?

An animal couldn't take away our sin since we are not animals; this could only cover the sin temporarily. We are made in God's image, very different from the animals. We have a spirit — the real person — that resides in our body. Our spirit will live after death. Because a man brought sin into the world, a perfect man was needed to pay the penalty for sin, which was death. Jesus was the only one who could take our place.

God's own Son stepped into history to become a man, Jesus Christ the God-man — a member of Adam's family. But God's Son was a perfect man — perfect and without sin. He would sacrifice Himself to save us. He died on a cross to pay the penalty for our sin (remember the penalty was death). He rose from the dead, paying for our sin and conquering death.

Jesus offers a free gift of salvation for those who will put their trust in Him as Savior and Lord of their life. Now those who have received God's free gift of salvation can live with Him forever when they die! This is the best and most important message in the entire universe! Jesus was the plan to save mankind from Adam's sin of disobedience.

Sin also changed Adam and Eve's lives in very real ways. They were driven from the garden and kept away by angels placed at the entrance so they could never return. The original harmony of their marriage was broken. Adam would have to work hard for his survival, growing food and finding shelter for him and his family. Now in a world stained by sin, they also faced dangers from the harshness of the weather and wild animals. And since he was formed from dust, he would return to dust when his physical body died.

The history of Adam and Eve is really our own history — trying to overcome a sinful nature, trying to survive in a world that now has death and illness and sorrow. Because of their sin, they could no longer live in the perfect Garden of Eden — and the world we live in is nothing close to perfect.

They would have children, but this joyous moment would be marred by Eve's pain in childbirth, and the later suffering brought about by their son Abel's murder by his own precious brother, Cain. Imagine the moment Adam and Eve realized the actual results of their sin — that their choice opened the door to this terrible tragedy.

*T*hings would not get much better for mankind. At one point the world was so filled with sin that it was all people thought of all the time. God again would judge the world for this sinful nature, sending a global flood that would destroy the world. Eight people — the family of one God-honoring man named Noah — would be saved along with the animals kind.

As terrible as parts of Adam and Eve's lives may have been and later the Flood itself, God still gave us hope for something better. The Bible tells how God sent His Son, the Lord Jesus Christ, who became a perfect man, so He could die on a cross for our sins. He had to die, because death was the penalty for sin given in the Garden of Eden. God the Father showed He accepted Christ's sacrifice as payment for our sin in that He raised the Lord Jesus from the dead.

So now, if you come to the Lord Jesus, and . . . "you confess with your mouth the Lord Jesus and believe in your heart that God has raised Him from the dead, you will be saved" (Romans 10:9). When we trust in the Lord Jesus and receive the free gift of salvation, God the Father sees our sins covered by what Jesus did on the Cross. This was the "picture" that God gave Adam and Eve when He clothed them in animal skins. This is called the gospel message — the message we are to preach to the whole world: "And He said to them, 'Go into all the world and preach the gospel to every creature'" (Mark 16:15). Now you can live with hope and joy even in the midst of a fallen world, because of God's grace.

Did you know the first time the gospel was actually preached is in the first book of the Bible — Genesis? Here is what God said concerning the battle between Satan, and the Lord Jesus, and that Jesus would be the victor over Satan so we could be saved from our sin: "And I will put enmity between you and the woman, And between your seed and her Seed; He shall bruise your head, And you shall bruise His heel" (Genesis 3:15).

We need to share this good news to every tribe and nation, because everyone is a descendant of Adam and Eve. We are all members of the human race (the human family) — just one race, and not different races as evolutionists once claimed. Thus, everyone is a sinner who needs Jesus Christ.

In the New Testament, we read about God's Son conquering death to pay the penalty for our sin:

For as in Adam all die, even so in Christ all shall be made alive. But each one in his own order: Christ the firstfruits, afterward those who are Christ's at His coming. Then comes the end, when He delivers the kingdom to God the Father, when He puts an end to all rule and all authority and power. For He must reign till He has put all enemies under His feet. The last enemy that will be destroyed is death (1 Corinthians 15:22–26).

We can again look forward to paradise and being with God forever because of Jesus. "And there shall be no more curse" (Revelation 22:3).... "And God will wipe away every tear from their eyes; there shall be no more death, nor sorrow, nor crying. There shall be no more pain, for the former things have passed away" (Revelation 21:4).

This sounds as if it will be just as it was in the Garden of Eden before sin — a perfect world where everything is "very good," and it will be good forever.

Can you now see how the history of Adam and Eve, and the results of their disobedience, is history that continues to impact the world throughout the Bible? From their disobedience to Jesus, His death on the Cross, and defeating death for us, plus the promise of eternity with God — it speaks again to the relevance of the Bible in our faith and daily lives. That's why it is so good to always have the Bible as our starting point and source for answers to any questions we or others may have.

Our Family from Adam to Noah

Number at left = age when son was born　　　Number at right = age of person at death

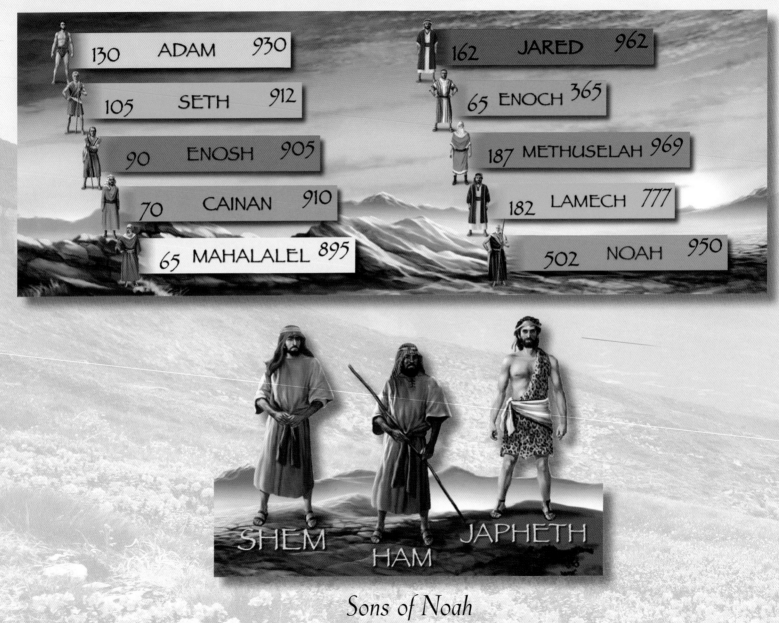

130	ADAM	930
105	SETH	912
90	ENOSH	905
70	CAINAN	910
65	MAHALALEL	895
162	JARED	962
65	ENOCH	365
187	METHUSELAH	969
182	LAMECH	777
502	NOAH	950

SHEM　HAM　JAPHETH

Sons of Noah

*A*nother very important question people often ask is "How long ago was it that God created Adam and Eve?" The Bible tells us a lot about Adam and Eve's family, including grandchildren, great-grandchildren, and more for many generations. Have you ever seen a family tree? It lists out everyone within a family who is related, and often will go back many years to record family history.

The Bible's very detailed family tree for Adam and Eve offers great detail like Adam was 130 years old he had a son named Seth, and that Adam lived to be 930 years old after having many sons and daughters. It also tells us that Seth was 105 he had his son Enosh, and Seth lived another 807 years. Enosh had a son named Cainan when he was 90 years old, and lived to be 905 years. This record continues through many generations.

Have you ever wondered why lists like this are all through the Bible? God did this so we could trace the history of the world back to the beginning! All these people were your relatives! Think about it! You have parents, and then they have parents (your grandparents), and they have parents (your great grandparents) — all the way back to Noah, and then all the way back to Adam. All people who have ever lived and who live today are all part of Adam's family!

When we add up all these dates in these family lists, and the dates of other events given in the Bible, we find that God created the universe, our world, and people around 6,000 years ago.

Two family lists in the Bible specifically mention Adam; one in the Old Testament (1 Chronicles 1:1–4) and another in the New Testament (Luke 3:38). These are always used as true records of history — lists of our relatives who were all part of Adam's family.

This means that Adam and Eve were created about 6,000 years ago! Jesus in the New Testament tells us that Adam and Eve were made at the beginning of creation referring to the sixth day — not billions of years after the universe came into existence like secular scientists try and tell us. It's important to be able to know that the Bible's timeline of history is correct. It speaks to the authority of the Bible over man-made ideas or theories that are different.

Did you know that there are over 7 billion people in the world today? Some people wonder how that many people could come from just two people 6,000 years ago. When you also take into account the Flood of Noah, a global disaster that reduced the population of the world 4,300 years ago to only 8 people, they ask, "Could so many people come from so few that fast?" Yes! If the population doubled only every 150 years, you would easily have the population we have currently.

Now this is a totally different view of history from the one we usually see on television, read in newspapers, or hear in almost all schools. Most of us have been bombarded with the idea that the universe came into existence billions of years ago, and life supposedly evolved over millions of years.

People who believe in evolution think humans began to evolve a couple of million years ago. Then what they call modern humans supposedly existed 200,000 years ago — and humans as we know them today supposedly began about 50,000 years ago! But if this really happened, and the population doubled only every 150 years, in just 50,000 years there would be what is called a *googol* number of people... that's a 1 followed by 100 zeroes! That just doesn't fit with what has happened. Just do the math! Only the Bible's history of beginning with eight people after the Flood just a few thousand years makes sense of the population numbers today.

Noah's Family During the Flood

Population doubles

every 150 years

to reach our population today.

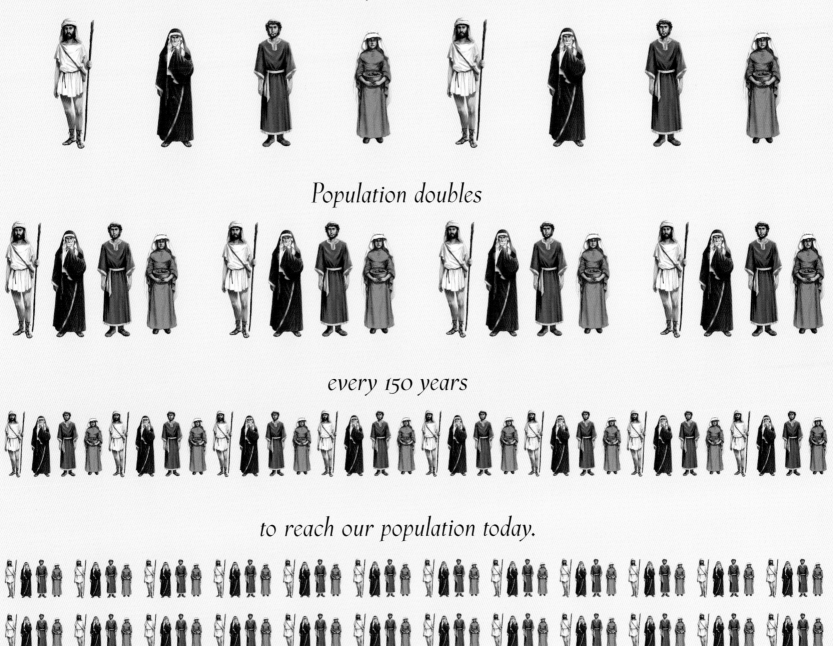

Conclusion

Now you know a lot more about the history of Adam and Eve! It makes more sense when you read their history in the Bible and realize they were real people, like you and me, whose lives changed when they made a choice to sin. When you hear people talking about Adam not being a real person and Genesis not being real history, you can know and tell others the truth that the Bible tells us about the first two people created by God. We all stand at a crossroads like Adam and Eve... and we all must individually make that decision to receive Christ and the wonders of His glory, or reject Him and in that way choose a life forever separated from His goodness and enduring His wrath for sin.

A lot of people assume that Adam is only really mentioned in the Old Testament or mostly just in Genesis. The Bible mentions Adam by name in nine different books! It is so obvious that Adam was a real person! In fact, he was our great, great, great, great.......... (and many more greats) grandparent, 6,000 years ago. You can look up these passages of Scripture to read more about the first man who would be the first person on all our family trees:

Genesis 1–5 – Deuteronomy 32:8

When the Most High divided their inheritance to the nations, When He separated the sons of Adam, He set the boundaries of the peoples According to the number of the children of Israel.

1 Chronicles 1:1–4 (Genealogy)

Adam, Seth, Enosh, Cainan, Mahalalel, Jared, Enoch, Methuselah, Lamech, Noah, Shem, Ham, and Japheth.

Job 31:33

If I have covered my transgressions as Adam, By hiding my iniquity in my bosom,

Luke 3:38

the son of Enosh, the son of Seth, the son of Adam, the son of God. (Genealogy)

Romans 5:12–14

Therefore, just as through one man sin entered the world, and death through sin, and thus death spread to all men, because all sinned—(For until the law sin was in the world, but sin is not imputed when there is no law. Nevertheless death reigned from Adam to Moses, even over those who had not sinned according to the likeness of the transgression of Adam, who is a type of Him who was to come.

1 Corinthians. 15:22

For as in Adam all die, even so in Christ all shall be made alive.

1 Corinthians 15:45

And so it is written, "The first man Adam became a living being."
The last Adam became a life-giving spirit.

1 Timothy 2:13-14

For Adam was formed first, then Eve. And Adam was not deceived,
but the woman being deceived, fell into transgression.

Jude 14

Now Enoch, the seventh from Adam, prophesied about these men also,
saying, "Behold, the Lord comes with ten thousands of His saints,

Ken Ham

A favorite at homeschooling and church conferences, Ken Ham is also the founder and president of *Answers in Genesis-U.S.* and the *Creation Museum*, as well as one of the most in-demand Christian speakers internationally. Ken's emphasis is on the relevance and authority of the book of Genesis and how compromise on Genesis has opened a dangerous door regarding how the culture and church view biblical authority. Ken has also authored over 25 books.

blog.answersingenesis.org | facebook.com/aigkenham | twitter.com/aigkenham

Bill Looney

Bill is the visionary talent behind some of the most unique Christian titles available today, creating illustrations in a variety of styles and mediums that bring to life projects like *Dinosaurs for Kids* and *The True Story of Noah's Ark*. He was formally schooled in all media beginning in public school, to The University of Texas at Arlington, Dallas Art Institute. Bill is proficient in all media, ranging from airbrush, oils, acrylics, pen & ink, watercolor, sculpture, and computer illustration.

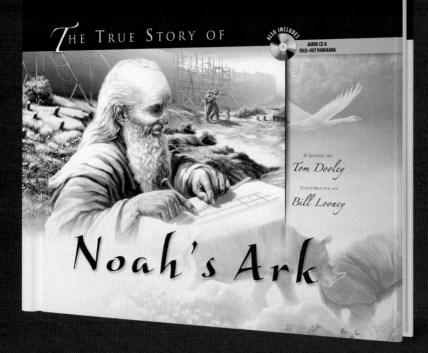

CONNECTING CHRISTIANS
who believe in Biblical Creation.

forums | blogs | groups | resources | and more!

CreationConversations.com